D1742485

THROW OPEN THE DOORS

The World Health Organization Framework Convention on Tobacco Control

Gary Johns

Australian Institute for Progress

Connor Court Publishing

The World Health Organization Framework Convention on Tobacco Control is a closed shop. It suffers strategic and resource weaknesses. The result is more harm to tobacco consumers than would otherwise be the case.

As long as the sole strategy is supply and demand reduction and the dominant tactic is to use exclusion to silence debate, little progress will be evident. These weaknesses can be overcome by throwing open the doors of the Convention to all interested parties.

Published in 2016 by Connor Court Publishing Pty Ltd

Copyright © Gary Johns 2016

All rights reserved. No part of this book may be reproduced
or transmitted in any form or by any means, electronic or
mechanical, including photocopying, recording or by any
information storage and retrieval system, without prior
permission in writing from the publisher.

Connor Court Publishing Pty Ltd
PO Box 7257
Redland Bay QLD 4165

sales@connorcourt.com
www.connorcourt.com
Phone 0497 900 685

ISBN: 978-1-925501-25-4

Front Cover Design: Maria Giordano

Front Cover Photo: istockphoto.com, used with permission

Printed in Australia

OUTLINE

I Argument

- *Background*

- *The Convention is not performing like other UN conventions*

- *Harm reduction should not be ignored*

- *Exclusion drives a narrow agenda*

- *The Convention has resource and expertise problems*

- *Promises and prevalence diverge*

II Recommendations

1. *All relevant State ministers must be fully engaged in COP 7 preparations*

2. *All relevant State and international regulators must be fully engaged in COP 7 preparations*

3. *All interested parties must be allowed to observe the COP 7 proceedings, as is standard procedure with other United Nations conferences*

4. *Parties at COP 7 should re-visit Article 1 of the Convention and recommence debate on the best means of achieving the Convention's aims*

5. *Parties and the FCTC Secretariat should undertake a renewal of engagement with all parts of the industry with a view to a realistic assessment of the shortest path to least harm, and all other matters of concern.*

III   Further evidence

- *Article 5.3 pretends to be law, and seeks to silence ...*

- *Article 5.3 has been used to censor officials and members of parliament*

- *Convention excludes expertise and resources*

IV Author's Biography and Publications

V About the Australian Institute for Progress

I
Argument

Background

The 2005 World Health Organization Framework Convention on Tobacco Control (Convention) is the first treaty negotiated under the auspices of the United Nations World Health Organization (WHO). Although extensive powers are vested in WHO to protect and promote international public health, including the preparation of conventions, the WHO had never wielded its treaty making power until this one.

In 1998 Dr Gro Harlem Brundtland, the WHO director-general, and former Norwegian Minister for Environmental Affairs, established the Tobacco Free Initiative under Dr Derek Yach. Brundtland argued, "Tobacco control cannot succeed solely through the efforts of individual governments, national non-governmental organisations and media advocates. We need an international response to an international problem."[1]

---

[1] WHO FCTC, 2009. *History of the WHO Framework Convention on Tobacco Control*, 6.

The Initiative was a vehicle to promote the Convention among WHO member States. In time, 180 State Parties agreed to be bound by the Convention. Each two years a conference of the Parties meets to report progress among member States in implementing the Convention.

The seventh Conference of the Parties to the Convention will take place at New Delhi 7-14 November 2016 (COP 7). In the light of strategies and tactics undertaken by WHO, the Parties, and the Convention Secretariat in the years since its establishment, it is time to assess progress.

The Convention is not performing like other UN conventions

The Convention's major strategic challenge is to open its doors to any and all sources of advice and assistance. The evidence presented here suggests that the Convention has become a closed shop. It has shunned advice that it does not want to hear. As a consequence, the Secretariat does not have the expertise or resources to deal with two big challenges of the Convention: finding a path for reduced harm alternatives to smoking, and tackling illicit trade in tobacco, which is caused by high and/or inconsistent taxation across borders, poor regulation, and poor policing. The result is poor public policy. Openness will not weaken its deliberations; indeed, the best policy outcomes demand openness.

The UN has learned the lessons of lack of legitimacy that stems from opaque decision-making. Over time it has embraced openness. The Convention, its Parties and Secretariat have not learned the lessons. Their restrictive behaviour is not the norm for UN debate. The United Nations welcomed world leaders, the media, external stakeholders and the public to the Paris Climate Change Conference in November 2015. Unlike Paris, the UN under the auspices of the WHO, will convene an international gathering for COP 7, which will be a meeting where the public, media, industry, law enforcement and other key external stakeholders may be barred from entry.

At COP 5, Parties raised concerns over the numbers of tobacco industry representatives among public attendees. As a result, a decision was made to exclude members of the public at some meetings. At COP 6, essentially two proposals to control attendance were canvassed, each of them Orwellian. First, the public would be required to sign a written declaration affirming that they were not affiliated with the tobacco industry; if they were affiliated then they would not be issued a badge.[2] Second, was a proposal to create a new type of meeting during COPs, called "open meetings", which would exclude members of the public but allow favoured observers.[3] In fine diplomatic style, the two proposals were referred to a committee that recommended 'consideration to providing options for maximizing transparency with regard to Party delegations, to COP and subsidiary bodies.'[4] The recommendation was duly adopted for application at COP 7. Its meaning is becoming apparent as COP 7 draws close.

The registration requirements for COP 7 will be heavily scrutinised for any connection between the industry and observers and member delegates. Members of the public who wish to observe these publicly funded proceedings will be forced to declare their affiliation. Anyone, including party delegates, that is, those who represent nations who pay for the Convention, would be excluded if they have contact with the tobacco industry. It is reported that the COP 7 organisers want to exclude representatives from 'state-owned tobacco industries' and 'certain appointed and

[2] WHO FCTC, Sixth Session Moscow, 2014. 'Attendance of members of the public in meetings of the Conference of the Parties to the WHO FCTC and its subsidiary bodies.' *Provisional agenda item 6.7*, 6.
[3] WHO FCTC, Sixth Session Moscow, 2014. *Verbatim Records Of Plenary Meetings*, 22.
[4] WHO FCTC, Sixth Session Moscow, 2014. *Verbatim Records Of Plenary Meetings*, 80.

elected officials from executive, legislative and judicial branches'.[5] This will be tough on those countries that have state controlled tobacco companies, or officials who need to deal with tobacco companies on taxation and illicit trade in tobacco, or media representatives who have to report on the industry, or the common taxpayer, or heaven forbid, smokers.

By contrast, the Paris Climate Change Conference hosted 3,000 accredited journalists. At both the Convention's COP 5 and COP 6 delegates agreed to remove journalists from plenary sessions. Paris had clear media inquiry contact points. Paris provided a constantly updated online news-hub, providing updates on decisions and activity, while also providing an e-mail news update feature. COP 6 did none of this.

The Paris Conference posted publicly available drafts of the key texts negotiated at the meeting. The Convention does not do this. Paris provided extensive webcasts of sessions, debates and press conferences and published webcasts of meetings held in preparation for the event. The Convention provides no such window into its decision-making process. Decisions were posted after the fact with no context as to how they were reached.

The UN Environment Programme hosted the *Sustainable Innovations Forum 2015* in conjunction

---

[5] Yael Ossowski, 'UN anti-tobacco meeting seeks to ban high-ranking government officials.' *Huffington Post* 11 August 2016.

with Paris. The forum brought together a diverse
range of business, finance, associations, international
organisations and media to discuss new and emerging
technologies and businesses strategies for addressing
climate change. The Convention prohibits any
involvement from external stakeholders and industry,
going so far as to ban Interpol from attending COP
6, despite that organisations expertise in combatting
the illegal tobacco trade (a key provision in the
Convention).

The Convention will not permit any discussion
or presentation on any matter by tobacco farmers,
tobacco companies, consumers, or anybody who may
raise divergent views of harm reduction and efforts to
develop new products. For example, The Federation
of All India Farmer Association has urged the Indian
government to have representation of tobacco farmers
at the COP 7.[6] Paris allowed organisations representing
a diverse range of ideological perspectives (from
ardent climate change activists to climate sceptics) to
attend the meeting. The Convention bars all outside
participation save for a select group of anti-tobacco
organisations that are fully supportive of its agenda.

According to the official Paris website, 'to prompt
a large number of people to participate and get

---

[6] 'Tobacco farmers seek participation in Global Tobacco control sum-
mit.' http://www.newkerala.com/news/2016/fullnews-100542.html
accessed 26 August 2016.

information, France has decided to build a dedicated space for civil society right next to the Conference Centre. This vast space will host debates, conferences, cultural exhibitions, film screenings, as well as stands presenting civil society solutions to climate change.'[7] The Convention does not do this.

The United Nations engagement with stakeholders and civil society can never be a substitute for national constituencies and elected officials, who provide democratic accountability. It must, therefore, always be open to scrutiny.[8] To be both removed from national constituencies and be a closed shop is fatal to good public policy. As Clive Bates, former Director of ASH United Kingdom, an anti-smoking Non-government Organisation (NGO), has stated, 'One wonders about the integrity of a process that is so fragile that it cannot tolerate dissenting voices.'[9] Openness and effectiveness should be the Convention measure of success, not the intensity of dislike for opponents.

---

[7] Paris 2015 UN Climate Change Conference, http://www.cop21.gouv. fr/en accessed 30 July 2016.

[8] Johns, G, 2004. 'Relations with nongovernmental organizations: lessons for the UN.' *Seton Hall Journal of Diplomacy and International Relations* Summer/Fall 51-65.

[9] Clive Bates, 'WHO plans e-cigarette offensive.' *The Counterfactual* 17 April 2014.

Harm reduction should not be ignored

As for effectiveness, the Convention has to wonder that, after all of its work, smoking persists. The prevalence of tobacco smoking among nations and demographic groups appears to follow a well-trodden path of rise and decline as nations develop, tastes change and consumers are better informed of the risks associated with tobacco consumption.[10] Significant reductions in smoking rates have been achieved in the United Kingdom, Australia, Brazil, and other countries. However, growing consumption in China and developing countries has offset these.[11] The Parties needs to assess the Convention strategy knowing that a very large number of people will choose to continue to consume tobacco, indeed, the WHO estimates that there is likely to be at least one billion smokers by 2025.[12]

Under the Convention, tobacco control means 'a range of supply, demand and harm reduction strategies that aim to improve the health of a population by eliminating or reducing their consumption of tobacco

---

[10] Lopez A, Collishaw N and Piha T, 1994. 'A descriptive model of the cigarette epidemic in developed countries.' *Tobacco Control* 3 242–7.

[11] *The Tobacco Atlas*, http://www.tobaccoatlas.org/topic/cigarette-use-globally/ accessed 15 July 2016.

[12] Bilano V et al, 2015. 'Global trends and projections for tobacco use, 1990–2025.' *The Lancet* 385 (9972), 966.

products.'[13] However, as Dr Derek Yach, whom the former DG of the WHO entrusted to commence the Convention, has pointed out, 'The importance of harm reduction as a critical part of future tobacco control was recognized and is thus included in Article 1 of the FCTC.'[14]

To be clear, harm reduction is not elsewhere mentioned in the Convention, which suggests hostility to the strategy at the outset. At the outset there was an understandable zeal to eliminate tobacco consumption. But that goal was always flawed. Despite advice to the contrary,[15] the WHO has pursued a single strategy of supply and demand reduction. It seems to have shunned a second strategy, which is to reduce the harm of smoking.[16] Undoubtedly, 'deep distrust by many in the tobacco control movement' has driven a 'reluctance to acknowledge the differential health risks [that] smokeless tobacco products could play in

---

[13] World Health Organization, 2005. *WHO Framework Convention on Tobacco Control*, 4.

[14] Derek Yach, 'Effective global tobacco control: time to engage health professionals, listen to smokers, and support harm reduction.' *Vitality Global* 26 February 2016.

[15] Stratton K et al, 2001. 'Clearing the smoke: the science base for tobacco harm reduction.' *Tobacco Control* 10(2) 189-95. Zeller M and Hatsukami D, 2009. 'The strategic dialogue on tobacco harm reduction: a vision and blueprint for action in the US.' *Tobacco Control* 18(4) 324–32. Nutt D J et al, 2014. 'Estimating the harms of nicotine-containing products using the MCDA approach.' *European Addiction Research* 20(2) 218-225.

[16] WHO urged the Parties at COP 6 2014, 'to consider banning or restricting advertising, promotion and sponsorship of electronic nicotine delivery systems ENDS.'

a harm reduction strategy.'[17] But embracing debate on differential risks among tobacco and nicotine products is likely to be a more promising strategy than hoping that all smokers will heed the call of the Convention and quit.

Under any realistic policy settings, it is entirely likely that tobacco smoking will remain a feature of human consumption, especially in some cultures, for example, China and Eastern and Southern Europe, and among certain parts of all societies, for example, lower socioeconomic groups.[18] A strategy that ignores harm reduction in the hope of eliminating smoking is grievously flawed. Moreover, it appears that the 'elimination' strategy is itself running into trouble because, as one researcher has observed, 'there is little relationship between tobacco control … and prevalence.'[19] If the elimination strategy is in doubt and harm prevention strategies have been avoided it is vital that, prior to COP 7, delegates are encouraged to think about opening debate on the lowest cost-most likely route to least harm.[20]

The Convention Secretariat is not taking the harm

---

[17] McNeill A, Hammond D and Gartner C, 2012. 'Whither tobacco product regulation?' *Tobacco Control*, 21(2) 225.

[18] *The Tobacco Atlas*, http://www.tobaccoatlas.org/topic/cigarette-use-globally/ accessed 15 July 2016.

[19] Clive Bates, 'Are you being manipulated? The wisdom of the WHO examined.' *The Counterfactual* 2 June 2013.

[20] Clive Bates, 'WHO plans e-cigarette offensive.' *The Counterfactual* 17 April 2014.

prevention route because it seems inured to the reality that the industry remains profitable and is unlikely to disappear even under the most stringent control regime.[21] The Secretariat seems oblivious to the fact that developed nations had already commenced tobacco reduction programs before the Convention was voted in, and developing nations are struggling to implement its provisions and rely on funds from developed nations, either taxpayers or philanthropists.[22] The Convention and its Secretariat are fighting the last war. The Convention has to ask itself: what is it doing for one billion smokers?

Exclusion drives a narrow agenda

The underlying principle of Article 5.3 of the Convention, which is to ensure that the industry does not unduly influence tobacco control policies, is understandable. But the Secretariat goes as far as to consider that even open discussions and exchange of views, which represents a cornerstone of good policy making in modern democracies, is problematic. As a result, the Secretariat uses Article 5.3 as an instrument

---

[21] MSCI, 2016, *World Tobacco Index*.
[22] Institute for Health Metrics and Evaluation, *Financing Global Health 2013*, 39.

to halt discussions altogether, including discussions of a wider risk strategy that could include harm reduction and realistic resourcing of anti-illicit trade strategies.

Rather than an open agenda, the Secretariat has pursued tactics, the evidence for which is set out in part III of this paper, which excludes technically proficient advisors, legitimate voices in the industry, and avoids public scrutiny. Article 5.3 of the Convention is a strong illustration of, and possible cause for, the failure of the Secretariat and the Parties to come to grips with the consumer marketplace, the unintended consequences of supply reduction, such as illicit trade, and the inadequate consideration given to the harm prevention side of the Convention.

Article 5.3 states that 'Parties shall act to protect [tobacco control] policies from commercial and other vested interests of the tobacco industry in accordance with national law.'[23] The guidelines, published by the Secretariat to elaborate Article 5.3, are highly inflammatory.

The tobacco industry has operated for years with the express intention of subverting the role of governments and of WHO in implementing public health policies to combat the tobacco epidemic.

Parties need to be alert to any efforts by the tobacco industry to undermine or subvert tobacco control efforts and the need to be

---

[23] WHO FCTC, 2005, 7.

informed of activities of the tobacco industry that have a negative impact on tobacco control efforts.[24]

The Secretariat and the Parties seem unable to appreciate that the 'industry' consists of consumers, taxpayers, regulators, and tobacco corporations, all operating in a legal framework. The Secretariat appears to speak only to those whom it regards as its allies in a crusade to eliminate a harmful, yet legal, product.

The Convention is most unlikely to succeed in the elimination of tobacco consumption. Bhutan is held out as an example of total 'control' because it has banned the sale of tobacco products. But even here, tobacco may be imported for personal consumption, and while only 3.5 per cent of people in Bhutan smoke, 43 per cent consume smokeless tobacco in the form of Betal quid and chewing tobacco.[25] It is to be hoped that reports of a ban on tobacco in the 'highly authoritarian' Turkmenistan,[26] and a WHO FCTC meeting that took place there in April 2016, do not suggest that the Convention has veered down an authoritarian path in order to reach its goals of tobacco control.[27]

---

[24] WHO FCTC, 2008. *Guidelines for Implementation of Article 5.3*, 1.

[25] Tobacco Control Laws, http://www.tobaccocontrollaws.org/legislation/country/bhutan/summary accessed 15 July 2016.

[26] Central Intelligence Agency, 2016. *The World Fact Book*. https://www.cia.gov/library/publications/the-world-factbook/geos/tx.html accessed 15 July 2016.

[27] Matt Broomfield, 'Turkmenistan president outlaws all sale of tobacco products, effectively banning smoking altogether.' *Independent* 17 January 2015.

Much of the Secretariat's energy is focussed on Article 5.3, which it uses as an instrument to halt discussion of a wider risk strategy that should include harm reduction and realistic resourcing of anti-illicit trade strategies. The Secretariat and various NGOs have taken numerous actions in many forums to shut down debate. For example,

- *Department of Health and Ageing, Australia*

- *Department of Justice, Republic of the Philippines*

- *The German Federal Government*

- *The High Court of Delhi, New Delhi*

- *The European Ombudsman, Brussels*

- *District Court of The Hague, The Netherlands*

In each case, courts of law or government officials, have confirmed that Article 5.3 does not have the effect of banning contact between the tobacco industry and government. Nevertheless, although unsuccessful as a legal instrument against government (the details of each decision are set out in part III of the paper), Article 5.3 has been used to empower NGOs and public health advocates to promote preferred strategies. The use and abuse of Article 5.3 has had the effect of passing power from decision-makers in government to a group who cannot do the job because they are remote from responsible state regulators and in conflict with experienced international agencies.

NGOs are not the sole source of knowledge in the field. Nor are they a substitute for public voice and, in any event, are not signatories to the Convention. Secretariat behaviour is a reflection on the Parties who have failed in their stewardship of taxpayer's funds, which pay for the Secretariat, in effect, subcontracting stewardship to remote and unelected officials and NGOs.

The Convention has resource and expertise problems

The Convention sits within the WHO program, which has to contend with a heavy burden of duties, and is in the throws of a reorganisation.[28] For the first time the 194 members of the World Health Assembly will vote to choose the leader of WHO, who will formally commence duties in July, 2017.[29] Whether a change

[28] Clift C, 2014. 'What's the World Health Organization for?' *Final Report from the Centre on Global Health Security Working Group on Health Governance*, The Royal Institute of International Affairs.

[29] Laurie Garrett, 'Secret vote on WHO bodes ill for future of global health.' *Humanosphere* 23 May 2016.

at the top can counteract the tendency for the WHO to continue to pursue its 'heroic' mandate, with its duplication of others work, lack of feasibility, and questionable impact, is moot.[30] Convention failings may, in part, stem from WHO governance, but for the most part are more mundane. It has few funds, lacks 'expertise and capacity to deal with illicit trade', and has failed to 'embed a multi-lateral approach to illicit trade within the existing international law enforcement and customs infrastructure.'[31]

The Convention and the Secretariat need to open up, indeed the Convention suggests this approach. There are a number of guiding principles, general obligations and measures in the Convention, some of which have been forgotten in the Secretariat's narrow purview. In particular, to use all available expertise, especially in taxation and customs:

Guiding Principles Article 4.3. International cooperation, particularly transfer of technology, knowledge and financial assistance and provision of related expertise, to establish and implement effective tobacco control programmes.

General Obligations Article 5.5. The Parties shall cooperate, as appropriate, with competent international and regional

---

[30] Hoffman, S and Rottingen J, 2013. 'Dark sides of the proposed framework convention on global health's many virtues.' *Health and Human Rights Journal* 15(1).

[31] Liberman J, 2012. 'Four COPS and counting: achievements, under-achievements and looming challenges in the early life of the WHO FCTC Conference of the Parties.' *Tobacco Control* 21(2) 216.

intergovernmental organizations and other bodies ...

Price and Tax Measures Article 6.1. The Parties recognize that price and tax measures are an effective and important means of reducing tobacco consumption by various segments of the population.[32]

Nowhere is technical expertise more important than in combatting illicit trade in tobacco. The Protocol to Eliminate Illicit Trade in Tobacco Products is the first protocol to the Convention, and a new international treaty in its own right.[33] The Protocol builds upon and complements Article 15 of the Convention, which addresses means of countering illicit trade in tobacco products.

Illicit Trade in Tobacco Products Article 15.4. .... each Party shall ... monitor and <u>collect data on cross-border trade</u> in tobacco products, including illicit trade, and exchange information among customs, tax and other authorities.[34] (author emphasis)

Supply Chain Control Article 8.1. For the purposes of further securing the supply chain and to assist in the investigation of illicit trade in tobacco products, the Parties agree to establish ... a global <u>tracking and tracing regime</u>.[35] (author emphasis)

The Protocol acknowledges the growth of international illicit trade in tobacco products, and that illicit trade both increases the accessibility

---

[32] WHO FCTC, 2005.

[33] Adopted 2012 at the fifth session of the COP, Seoul.

[34] WHO FCTC, 2005.

[35] WHO FCTC, 2013. *The Protocol to Eliminate Illicit Trade in Tobacco Products*, 15.

and affordability of tobacco products and causes substantial losses in government revenues.[36] Clearly, technical cooperation is essential, but the Secretariat has consciously eschewed cooperation with technically competent officials, despite the fact that the Protocol deems essential such cooperation.

In addition to the tobacco industry, the Secretariat and the Parties have at one time or another excluded from its meetings,

- *Interpol*

- *Customs*

- *Tobacco farmers*

- *Taxation experts*

- *Media*

The Convention has become the sole province of health ministers and WHO officials. Often, other ministers, such as treasury, finance and customs have been ignored. Experienced and expert national and international regulators are excluded from deliberations, and industry and the public, including the media, are excluded from observing Convention policy-making

---

[36] WHO FCTC, 2013, 1.

proceedings. The details of these exclusions are set out in part III of the paper.

The exclusion of industry and other expertise is harmful. It is naïve to think that the industry will cease to lobby government in its own interests but, in any event, this can hardly be construed as 'subverting the role of governments.' Just as they do with other industries, many governments are in constant contact with, and seek advice from, the tobacco industry. It is also naïve for Dr Margaret Chan, Director-General of WHO to lecture politicians about tobacco taxation 'Get your governments to raise taxes on tobacco products … Above all, fight against tax policies … that punish the poor',[37] knowing that politicians are both reluctant to punish the poor with taxes that are highly regressive, as are tobacco excises, and eager to receive revenue from those sources.

The Secretariat seems not to appreciate that it operates in a world where tobacco taxation is heavily contested, where the interests of tobacco corporations and governments are opposed in some regards, for example the level of taxation, and aligned in others, for example the consequences of taxation on illicit trade. These conflicts are multiplied in those nations where producers are government-owned.

The Secretariat wants to ban contact between

---

[37] Address at the 133rd Inter-Parliamentary Union Assembly Geneva, Switzerland, 19 October 2015.

NGOs and those who receive moneys from tobacco companies for legitimate services, for example, taxation, customs and surveillance advice. Indeed, the Secretariat has praised actions by those governments that have divested from tobacco,[38] and yet it is prepared to take money for their income from taxes on tobacco consumers. A proposal for a 'solidarity tobacco contribution' (STC) shows that the Convention shares with most bureaucracy a distinct propensity to self-preservation.

It should be appreciated that the Secretariat and its program are funded by 'voluntary' contributions of the Parties and that, as of 2016-17, these are less than $10 million per annum.[39] A 2011 WHO discussion paper floated the idea of a surcharge on national tobacco taxes, worth 'in excess of US$ 5.5 billion per year',[40] voluntarily passed to WHO as a 'a novel approach' to fund raising.'[41] Far from being a novel approach, the STC is nothing more than a tax on a tax.

[38] WHO FCTC, 'Examples of implementation of Article 5.3 communicated through the reports of the Parties.' For example, Norway: The Government pension fund may no longer invest in the tobacco production industry. http://www.who.int/fctc/parties_experiences/en/ accessed 15 July 2016.

[39] Currency unspecified. WHO FCTC, 2016. 'Status of payments of voluntary assessed contributions as of 31 March 2016.'

[40] In response to the recommendation made by the High Level Taskforce on Innovative Financing for Health Systems WHO, 2008. *Taskforce on Innovative International Financing for Health Systems*, 11.

[41] WHO, 2011. *The Solidarity Tobacco Contribution*, Discussion Paper, 4.

Promises and prevalence diverge

A great deal of the Secretariat's effort is focussed on gathering Parties' reports. The Secretariat is mandated to consider the implementation reports that Parties are obliged to submit and to produce an annual summary of reports. These reports convey little about what is happening in individual nations and the conclusions that can be drawn from them about the successes and challenges of implementation are very general.[42]

Merely signing the Convention is not tantamount to implementing its measures. It is a promise at best. For other parts of the Convention, Parties report progress on a regular basis, the latest in 2014. Although reporting steady progress, as of 2014, 27 per cent of Parties submitted no report whatsoever. The average implementation rate of the 'substantive' articles of the Convention 'approached' 60 per cent, which means that more than 40 per cent had not implemented the substantive provisions.[43]

Specifics are a different story again. Compliance with Supply Chain Control Article 8.1 of the Protocol 'tracking and tracing' is only 26 per cent, while 'collection of data on cross-border trade' is 53 per cent. Only 71 per cent of Parties have enacted legislation

---

[42] Liberman, 2012.

[43] WHO FCTC, 2014. *Global Progress Report on the Implementation of the WHO Framework Convention on Tobacco Control.*

against illicit trade.[44] The Protocol to Eliminate Illicit Trade in Tobacco Products is not as yet in force. As of August 2016, only 19 of 58 Signatories had ratified the Protocol.[45] It should also be appreciated that the US has not ratified the Convention and Indonesia has not signed the Convention.

This procedure appears to have deteriorated to a tick-the-box exercise on agreed measures of control in each nation. For example, the relationship between reporting control activities and prevalence reduction, and even more important, harm reduction, is very weak. The following observations from Clive Bates are in conjunction with the European ban on SNUS, used in Sweden as an alternative to tobacco smoking. Sweden scores well on smoking prevalence and low on cancers associated with tobacco, a much better record than UK and Ireland, but scores poorly on 'control activity', the tick-the-box compliance exercise the Convention encourages.

The UK and Ireland score highly on an index of tobacco control activity called the 'Tobacco Control Scale'.[46] The Index consists of scores and weightings for tobacco control measures, such as tax and price increases; bans on smoking in public places; consumer

---

[44] WHO FCTC, 2014, 45.

[45] United Nations Treaty Collection, *treaties.un.org* accessed 15 July 2016.

[46] For Europe see, Joossens L and M Raw, 2010. *The Tobacco Control Scale 2010 in Europe*. Association of European Cancer Leagues.

awareness campaigns; bans on advertising and promotion; prominence of health warnings; smoking cessation treatment and access to medicinal nicotine. Access to low-risk recreational nicotine alternatives to smoking is not assessed or recognised as part of tobacco control, so harm reduction does not count.[47]

---

[47] Bates, 2013.

II

Recommendations

The World Health Organization Framework Convention on Tobacco Control is a closed shop. It suffers strategic and resource weaknesses. The result is more harm to tobacco consumers than would otherwise be the case. Throughout the previous six COPs, the Convention has adopted a number of supply and demand reduction measures, while harm reduction remains untapped.

The strategies to eliminate smoking and others aimed at reducing the harm caused by smoking are not mutually exclusive. These strategies can complement each other, especially to ensure that those who are unwilling or unable to quit have less harmful options available.

As long as the sole strategy is supply and demand reduction and the dominant tactic is to use exclusion, specifically Article 5.3, to silence debate, little progress will be evident. These weaknesses can be overcome by

throwing open the doors of the Convention to all interested parties.

A more intelligent principle is to follow the shortest
path to the least harm.

A more realistic response to the market should
dictate that harm reduction measures become a second
focus of discussion, with all parties engaged.

A more open approach to deliberation would ensure
that all parts of government are involved in policy
formulation in each signatory nation.

A more mature approach to the entirety of the
issues would involve all parts of the industry.

Therefore,

Prior to the Conference of the Parties at New Delhi
7-14 November 2016, it is recommended that:

*1.   All relevant State ministers must be fully engaged
in COP 7 preparations*

*2.   All relevant State and international regulators
must be fully engaged in COP 7 preparations*

At the Conference of the Parties at New Delhi 7-14
November 2016, it is recommended that:

*3.   All interested parties must be allowed to observe
the COP 7 proceedings, as is standard procedure with*

other United Nations conferences

4.   Parties at COP 7 should re-visit Article 1 of the Convention and recommence debate on the best means of achieving the Convention's aims

Following the Conference of the Parties, it is recommended that:

5.   Parties and the FCTC Secretariat should undertake a renewal of engagement with all parts of the industry with a view to a realistic assessment of the shortest path to least harm, and all other matters of concern.

III

Further evidence

Article 5.3 pretends to be law, and seeks to silence ...

By contrast with those parts of the Convention (and Protocol) that reach out, Article 5.3 seeks to silence voices. Surprisingly, however, despite the express desire and aim to silence tobacco corporations, instead Article 5.3 has been used to silence many officials within governments, international agencies and expert individuals.

Numerous NGOs, encouraged by the Secretariat and using Article 5.3, have initiated legal challenges to exert Convention power over governments and government agencies and experts. These have not been successful at law, as legal decisions and official opinions below demonstrate, but nevertheless they have interfered with genuine consultation by parties who have a legitimate interest in policymaking.

Department of Health and Ageing, Australia, 30 March 2004

The Australian government is required to report to Parliament on any treaty it signs. The advice from the Departent of Health proposed that Australia take binding treaty action to ratify the World Health Organization Framework Convention on Tobacco Control in accordance with Article 35 of that Convention. It argued, nevertheless, that

Article 5 … obliges parties to guard against the inappropriate exercise of influence from the tobacco industry in relation to tobacco control. Standard industry consultation on matters of policy, such as is routinely undertaken in Australia, is not inappropriate under this Article.[48]

Department of Justice, Republic of the Philippines, 4 July 2011

The Secretary of the Department of Health sought legal opinion from the Department of Justice on the interpretation and application of Article 5.3. Anti-tobacco advocates raised the issue of conflict of interest with Philip Morris and other tobacco

---

[48]   Department of Health and Ageing, Australia, 'National interest analysis: category B treaty.' *Documents tabled in Parliament* 30 March 2004.

companies in the membership roll of the Philippine Business for Social Progress (PBSP), which was involved in the management of some health grants. The advice concluded that

The Philippine Government ... [is] not absolutely prohibited or precluded from entering into partnership with, or participating in activities of, those in the tobacco industry.

In the case of the PBSP, it must be noted that the body is a business-initiated, social development-focused foundation, made of business-oriented corporate entities that raise funds necessary for the implementation of development projects ... The membership, therefore, of Philip Morris and other tobacco companies in PBSP does not convert the body into a tobacco industry ... Rather, the body can be a perfect partner of the Department of Health in the implementation of the mandate and purpose of the FCTC.[49]

The German Federal Government, Reply to Members of the Bundestag, 16 May 2012

Members of the Bundestag sought answers as to why the Federal Government had not announced, among other things, 'measures to protect public-health policy from commercial and other vested interests of the

---

[49] Republika Ng Pilipinas Kagawaran Ng Katarungan, Department Of Justice, Manila, *Opinion No. 28*, Series of 2011, 4 July 2011.

tobacco industry (Guidelines for Implementation of Article 5.3 of the FCTC)'. The reply, sent on behalf of the Federal Government in a letter by the Federal Ministry for Public Health, stated

The Guidelines for Implementation of the WHO Framework Convention on Tobacco Control are to be understood as offers to the Parties to implement the Convention in the best possible way in accordance with national conditions. They represent options for action. Therefore, a signatory state is not required to take up every one of these recommendations.[50]

The High Court of Delhi, New Delhi, 1 May 2015

An Indian NGO, *The Institute of Public Health*, petitioned the court for an injunction against the Ministry of Finance, Ministry of Health and Family Welfare of the Union of India and Government of National Capital Territory of Delhi to prevent ministry officials attending, and/or providing assistance to the 12th Annual Asia-Pacific Tax Forum May, 2015 co-organized by the International Tax and Investment Center at New Delhi. The court dismissed the petition because

---

[50] Deutscher Bundestag, *17th Electoral Period.* 21 May, 2012, Print No. 17/9706.

The Court cannot tell the Government how to go about its conduct and business on a day-to-day basis … It cannot be lost sight of that we are a democratic country and where the government, comprising of representatives of people, is answerable to the people for its actions … Such representatives of people are supposed to know and be aware of the needs of the people and what is good and bad for them.[51]

The European Ombudsman, Brussels, 1 October 2015

The NGO, *Corporate Europe Observatory*, complained to the Ombudsman that the European Commission was not meeting its obligation, under the Convention, to be accountable and transparent in its dealings with the tobacco industry. In particular, the complaint was that the Commission (with the exception of Director General Health) was failing to proactively publish details and minutes of meetings with representatives of the tobacco industry.

The Commission's position was that, by dealing with applications for access to documents concerning meetings with the tobacco industry, and by responding to relevant questions from Members of the European

---

[51] High Court of Delhi at New Delhi, *Institute Of Public Health versus Union Of India and Ors*, 1 May, 2015 W.P.(C) 4402/2015, 11.

Parliament, it was meeting its obligation under the Convention to be accountable and transparent.

The Ombudsman took the view that parties to the Convention are required to take active measures both to limit the extent of interactions with the tobacco industry and to ensure transparency where such interactions occur. The Ombudsman recommended to the Commission that all of its Directorates should ensure proactive transparency.[52] In other words, Article 5.3 does not disallow meetings between the Commission and tobacco industry representatives.

District Court of The Hague, The Netherlands, 9 November 2015

The Dutch foundation, *Stichting Rookpreventie Jeugd*, sought to invoke Article 5.3, and its accompanying Guidelines, to restrain the Dutch government from any dealings with the tobacco industry. The foundation requested a declaratory judgment stating, among other things, that the State was failing to comply with its obligations under Article 2 of the European Convention for the Protection of Human Rights and

---

[52] European Ombudsman, 'Recommendation of the European Ombudsman in the inquiry into complaint 852/2014/LP against the European Commission regarding its compliance with the Tobacco Control Convention.' 1 October 2015.

Fundamental Freedoms, and various UN Conventions, 'to the extent that it concerns the concrete realisation of these obligations as embodied in Article 5.3 …'

The Court concluded that 'Article 5.3 WHO Framework Convention has no direct effect' on Dutch law because 'Article 5.3 WHO Framework Convention and the result to be achieved with it have been described insufficiently precisely for them to serve as substantiation for the fundamental rights laid down' in the various Conventions invoked by the foundation.[53]

There is, perhaps, a clue in the judgement that were Article 5.3 to establish more concrete objectives (and the Dutch government remain a signatory), these may affect Dutch law. The Secretariat may seek to amend Article 5.3 by incorporating explicit obligations and standards, which would enhance its likelihood as an instrument to pursue the Parties. It is vital, therefore, that all interests within government are represented at the forthcoming COP 7 meeting.

Article 5.3 has been used to censor officials and members of parliament

The Convention is an example of 'networked' governance whereby many levels of government and

[53] District Court of The Hague, *Stichting Rookpreventie Jeugd versus The State of the Netherlands*, 9 November 2016, C/09/475711/Ha Za 14-1193, 14.

non-government interests cooperate for the greater good.[54] Unfortunately, and inevitably, some interests will be better organised than others and capture the instruments ceded by governments to international officials, who, in turn, use these to range across a very wide field of interests. Or, license NGOs to challenge national regulators in their own domain. There are numerous examples of such behaviour, including exclusion of industry representatives.

Industry observer excluded at a UN conference unrelated to health

A representative from Japan Tobacco International (JTI) was barred as a speaker at a meeting on investment policy hosted by the United Conference on Trade and Development (UNCTAD). Mr Ulle Geir, JTI director of international trade, was to speak at UNCTAD's biennial investment forum in Kenya on 19 July 2016.

In a letter to UNCTAD, Framework Convention Alliance NGO members, wrote 'strengthening implementation of the FCTC is one of the means of implementation targets included in the United Nations

[54] Saurer J, 2011. 'Supranational governance and networked accountability structures: member state oversight of EU agencies.' *European Journal of Risk Regulation* 2(1) 51-60.

Sustainable Development Goals that were adopted in September 2015.' They also wrote, 'Article 5.3 of the FCTC, requires governments to protect public health policies with respect to tobacco control from the commercial and other vested interests of the tobacco industry.'

In its letter, FCA called on UNCTAD, as well as other UN agencies and bodies, to help develop a policy on 'preventing tobacco industry interference', and to adopt it without delay. It also sought confirmation that, until such a policy is adopted, UNCTAD would put in place, structures and procedures to prevent any tobacco industry employee or representative from acting as a speaker or participant at any event organised by UNCTAD.[55]

European and Indian officials

The NGO collective, *Smoke Free Partnership*, wrote to Mr Heinz Zourek Director General for Tax and Customs Union European Commission quoting Article 5.3 and stating their concerns related to his announced participation to the Eurasia Tax Forum 2015 organised

[55] Framework Convention Alliance, http://www.fctc.org/media-and-publications/media-releases-blog-list-view-of-all-313/industry-interference/1428-advocates-gets-tobacco-industry-rep-removed-as-speaker-at-un-meeting accessed 26 August 2016.

by the International Tax and Investment Center in Brussels, on 1 July 2015.[56] Mr Zourek replied, 'I would like to assure you that the Commission takes its obligations as a party to the FCTC very seriously … I can confirm that my participation in the Eurasia Tax Forum will have no bearing whatsoever on the Commission policy regarding the implementation of public health policies with respect to tobacco control.'[57]

The *Institute of Public Health* may have lost its legal case against the Indian government (May 2015), but the State Minister and ministry officials withdrew from the event.[58] The World Bank decided not to participate or financially support the event, stating, 'The 12th Annual Asia Pacific Tax Forum had sought technical and financial support from the World Bank. However, after careful consideration, the bank has decided not to participate/financially support the event.'[59]

---

[56] Florence Berteletti, *Smoke Free Partnership*, letter 22 May 2015.

[57] The Director-General, *European Commission Directorate-General Taxation and Customs Union,* letter 19 June 2015.

[58] Abantika Ghosh, 'MoS, bureaucrats on guest list of tax meet funded by tobacco giants.' *The Indian Express* 29 April 2015.

[59] Sushmi Dey, 'World Bank exits event funded by tobacco companies.' *The Times of India* 2 May 2015.

Scottish Parliament

In 2014, ASH Scotland (which received more than
£425,000 of public funding in 2015 and similar
amounts in earlier years)[60] accused clerks to the
Economy, Energy and Tourism Committee of the
Scottish Parliament of contravening Article 5.3 by
sending committee members information from
KPMG on the illicit trade in tobacco in advance of one
of its meetings. ASH acknowledged that the 'FCTC
does not prohibit parties from engagement with the
tobacco industry', but still launched a public petition,
which was presented by ASH to the Public Petitions
Committee of the Parliament.[61]

The head of ASH Scotland, Sheila Duffy, was subject
to some strong criticism from Members:

Stewart Stevenson:

> ... *are [you] specifically asking the committee to support
> a petition that says that one sector of society has to be
> stripped of its ability to contact us in a way that everyone
> else takes for granted.*

---

[60] ASH (Scotland), *Financial Statements* 31 March 2015, 16.
[61] The Scottish Parliament, *Public Petition PE01580*.

Jackson Carlaw:

> *... parliamentary committees should be proscribed from hearing from the tobacco industry on a range of issues, which you say is mandated under the WHO treaty, to which we are a signatory?*

David Torrance:

> *You suggest that we cannot take evidence from somebody who represents a tobacco company or who is speaking on a tobacco company's behalf and that we cannot listen to their side of the argument ... Would you expect the same scrutiny to apply to ASH if it gave evidence to a committee?*

Stewart Stevenson:

> *Is the treaty (5.3) a form of censorship?*

Sheila Duffy (ASH Scotland):

> *To be honest, I think that it would save you time.*[62]

---

[62] Scottish Parliament, Official Report, Public Petitions Committee, *New Petitions International Health Treaty Standards (Guidance)* (PE1580), 10 November 2015, 20-24.

European Parliament

In 2011, anti-tobacco campaigners accused the European Parliament's Budgetary Affairs Committee of contravening Article 5.3 for taking evidence, in a public session, from a tobacco company on the subject of the illicit trade, in spite of the existence of an agreement between the company and EU Member States to tackle the illicit trade.[63] In 2013, health NGOs in Brussels claimed the then Commission President, Barroso, and his Cabinet were in breach of Article 5.3, even though the Commission had previously released relevant documents for public scrutiny.[64] In December 2015, the head of the FCTC Secretariat accused senior European Commission officials of violating Article 5.3 if they continued to talk to the tobacco industry about the illegal trade in cigarettes.[65]

In February 2016, *Smokefree Partnership* claimed that the European Commission's anti-illicit trade agreement

---

[63] Andrew Rowell and Anna Gilmore, 'European parliamentary committee and Japan Tobacco: a violation of article 5.3 of the FCTC?' *BMJ Blogs* 11 October 2012.

[64] Smoke Free Partnership, 'European public health and transparency organisations send a letter to Commission President Barroso asking for the consistent implementation of Article 5.3 of the Framework Convention on Tobacco Control,' *News* 17 January 2013.

[65] Quentin Ariès And James Panichi. 'United Nations agency gives EU a tobacco warning.' *Politico* 16 December 2015.

with tobacco companies contravened Article 5.3.[66] The
European Commission had repeatedly issued detailed
statements outlining why it was not in breach of
Article 5.3, and on this occasion responded especially
forcefully.[67] The Commission's technical assessment of
the PMI agreement concluded that [its] core objective
had been met effectively, reducing the prevalence of
PMI contraband on the illicit EU tobacco market by 85
per cent in the volume of genuine PMI cigarettes seized
by Member States between 2006 and 2014.[68] However,
the reduction of PMI contraband did not lead to an
overall reduction of illicit products on the EU market,
which suggests smugglers have found other products
or ways to smuggle onto the EU market.[69]

The European Commission has not renewed the
anti-smuggling agreement with tobacco firm PMI,[70]
despite the fact that, 'it is likely to receive support from
EU capitals' and the fact that the EU had 'no alternative

---

[66] Smoke Free Partnership, 'Health organisations outraged by EU's
"possible" decision to extend agreement with tobacco transnational
Philip Morris.' *SFP Joint Press release* 25 February 2016.

[67] European Parliament, Answer given by First Vice-President
Timmermans on behalf of the Commission. 2 December 2015.

[68] European Parliament, 2016. 'European Parliament resolution of 9 March
2016 on the tobacco agreement (PMI agreement)', (2016/2555(RSP)), 1.

[69] European Commission, 2016. 'Technical assessment of the experience
made with the Anti-Contraband and Anti-Counterfeit Agreement and
General Release of 9 July 2004 among Philip Morris International and
affiliates, the Union and its Member States.' *Commission Staff Working
Document,* Brussels, SWD (2016) 44, 4.

[70] Peter Teffer, 'EU ends anti-smuggling deal with tobacco firm PMI.' *EU
Observer* 6 July 2016.

mechanisms' to achieve the goals of the PMI deal.[71]

The Commission has declared its intention to focus on using 'EU and international legislative tools', which can only mean the Protocol.[72] The anti illicit trade Protocol will enter into force once ratified by 40 parties to the Convention. The trouble is the Secretariat has recently announced that the Protocol will not come into force, for the foreseeable future, because too few nations have signed up.[73]

However, there are some binding requirements from the Convention itself, including obligations to:

> *4. (a) monitor and collect data on cross-border trade in tobacco products, including illicit trade, and exchange information among customs, tax and other authorities*
>
> *...*
>
> *(b) enact or strengthen legislation, with appropriate penalties and remedies, against illicit trade in tobacco products, including counterfeit and contraband cigarettes*
>
> *...*
>
> *(d) adopt and implement measures to monitor, document and control the storage and distribution of tobacco*

---

[71] Peter Teffer, 'EU states "unlikely to block new tobacco deal".' *EU Observer* 13 April 2016.

[72] European Parliament News, 'Cigarettes: MEPs oppose renewing EU anti-smuggling deals with tobacco firms.' 9 March 2016.

[73] Dr Vera da Costa e Silva FCTC, 'The Convention Secretariat announces that MOP1 will not be held in conjunction with COP7.' Geneva, 12 August 2016. There are presently nineteen Parties to the Protocol, it requires 40 to come into effect.

*products held or moving under suspension of taxes and
duties within its jurisdiction.[74]*

As noted above, many countries are not fulfilling
these obligations, which is surprising considering that
the WHO estimates that approximately ten per cent
of the global cigarette market is illicit, and in some
countries it is above 50 per cent. It is estimated that
governments could gain US$30 billion a year in tax
revenue if it were eliminated.[75]

Local councils

In 2015, ASH wrote to every local government
authority in the UK to warn elected representatives
and officials that if they did not act in compliance with
Article 5.3 'legal proceedings [could be] brought by
an individual or other non-state body against a public
authority.' They warned that 'an authority that does not
act in compliance with the convention may be exposed
to risk of judicial review.'[76]

The Local Declaration on Tobacco Control was
developed by ASH in the run up to the transfer of

---

[74] WHO FCTC, 2013, 56.

[75] WHO FCTC, 2013, *Summary*, 5.

[76] Tackling Illicit Tobacco for Better Health, http://www.illegal-tobacco.
co.uk/problem/undermining-tobacco-control/guidance-trading-
standards/ accessed 15 July 2016.

public health services to local government during 2011-12.[77] The idea behind the Declaration was to protect local public health policies from the supposed undue influence of the tobacco industry following the transfer of public health. There has been no case proven where such undue influence has been exerted either nationally or locally in the UK. Arguably, it is in ASH's interest to perpetuate this myth for their own existence and funding as they derive £200,000 per annum from the Department of Health.

As a result, local authorities that have succumbed to lobbying and over-implemented Article 5.3, have lost access to resources and intelligence that previously allowed them to seize millions of pounds worth of illegal cigarettes: 'it is preventing the industry from working with signatory councils (trading standards) on the issue of the illegal trade in tobacco products, which cost the Exchequer £2.1 billion in 2014 alone, imposed significant costs on retailers as a result of lost sales, and brought organised criminal gangs into local communities.'[78]

---

[77] Action on Smoking and Health (Scotland), *Annual Review 2015*, 11.

[78] Harry Phibbs, 'Perverse outcomes of councils' anti-smoking policies.' *Conservative Home* 30 June 2015.

Convention excludes expertise and resources

Interpol

In 2012, at its COP meeting in Korea, the Parties voted to eliminate the illicit trade in tobacco. At the same meeting Interpol, the world's preeminent authority on organised crime, illicit trade and money laundering, was excluded on the grounds that it worked with the tobacco industry. The Parties 'rejected an application by Interpol to become an official observer at the COP because of concerns about Interpol's decision, announced in June 2012, to accept a €15 million donation from Philip Morris International. This rejection was both highly embarrassing to Interpol, and an important signal to governments, as the tobacco industry is widely expected to attempt to offer "technical assistance" for Protocol implementation.[79]

The Convention has failed to deliver on this objective and recently the illicit trade has increased and was recently cited by the US State Department as a source of terrorist funding. Even its allies have acknowledged the Convention's failure in this area, noting it has 'not yet come to grips with the implications of the lack of expertise and capacity in

---

[79] Francis Thompson (Framework Convention Alliance), 'Strengthening FCTC implementation: an overview from Seoul.' *BMJ Blogs* 27 November 2012.

the health sector to deal with illicit trade.'[80]

Customs

Typical of attacks on officials is that published in *Tobacco Control* by NGO activists. The World Customs Organization welcomed Elizabeth Allen to present a two-day module on excisable products and illicit trade. The 2015 meeting was the fourth consecutive year that the International Taxation and Investment Center had delivered the module. ITIC receives funds from, among others, tobacco corporations.

Ms Allen was roundly criticised by the NGO because, although previously a senior official in UK Customs and Excise, she wrote an ITIC report on illicit tobacco, *The Illicit Trade in Tobacco Products and How to Tackle It*.[81] (The Secretary General of the World Customs Organization wrote the foreword, and before publication staff at the European Anti Fraud Office, the US Department of Treasury and International Monetary Fund reviewed it). Allen responded that 'the article gives a wholly false and skewed view of the ITIC guidebook.'

---

[80] Liberman, 2012, 219.
[81] Middleton J and Mackay J (Clear the Air NGO, Hong Kong), 2016. 'Worldwide news and comment.' *Tobacco Control* 25(1).

As the former UK senior civil servant in a revenue authority who was privileged to lead the first UK Alcohol and Tobacco Fraud Review in 1997, my motivation in writing this guidebook has been to pass on my knowledge and experience of the illegal tobacco trade to assist officials in developing countries in improving their administration of excise taxation and anti-smuggling controls.

I have never sought to undermine tobacco control policies. Rather, I have sought to help the tax and enforcement authorities to reduce opportunities for illegal trade, reduce demand and detect and prosecute the criminals and terrorists who profit from illegal trade drawing heavily on the UK experience in successfully reducing illegal trade in tobacco products from over 20 per cent in 2000 to around 10 per cent currently whilst maintaining one of the highest tax rates in the world.

It is undeniable that products that are light, portable and subject to high levels of tax attract criminals ... there are, however, several drivers and facilitators of illegal trade in tobacco products including tobacco taxation policy, corruption, protectionist measures, inadequate legislation such as penalties, inadequate enforcement and public tolerance though it is my personal view that the economic drivers of supply and demand are the most important.

As a former administrator I was trained and required to treat all taxpayers fairly without favouring one industry or one company over another. This has to be a key feature of effective tax and customs administration all over the world. The tobacco industry is a significant payer of excise revenue – second only to the hydrocarbon oil industry – and as long as it sells legal products and complies with legislative requirements it deserves the same treatment as any other industry.

Seizure rates, even in those countries that pride themselves on top class enforcement, do not exceed 20 per cent ... and in the EU were around 7 per cent in 2011. Seizure rates can be expected to be considerably less in relation to illicit trade in most developing countries. So, enforcement authorities need all the help they can get from others in the public sector.[82]

Tobacco farmers

Another objective of the Convention is to end the cultivation of tobacco globally. The Convention proposes to regulate growing seasons, reduce the area that can be cultivated, restrict funding and support for farmers and prevent the registration of new farmers. Health officials have drawn up these proposals without any dialogue with ministries of agriculture or agricultural producer groups. The International Tobacco Growers Association has been refused entry to all public meetings held by the Convention on the basis that 'their activities may not be in line with the

---

[82] Allen E, 2016. 'Worldwide news and comment.' *Tobacco Control* 25(1).

aims and spirit of the Convention.'[83]

The third meeting of the working group was held in Geneva, Switzerland, February 2012. Key Facilitators and Partners of the working group attended and participants included representatives of WHO, the International Labour Organization, the Food and Agriculture Organization of the United Nations, and the United Nations Environment Programme, as well as representatives of NGOs accredited as observers to the COP and invited experts. But, there were no growers.[84] This, despite the fact that the Convention promulgated a Principle (2) that 'tobacco growers and workers should be involved in policy development'.[85]

The meeting of the Parties has refused to deal with the World Farmers' Organisation and excluded it from its meetings, voting in COP 6 (2014) to refuse observer status (along with refusing Interpol).[86] And yet, a spokesperson for Corporate Accountability International and the Network for Accountability of Tobacco Transnational 'and a network of more than 50 NGOs around the world dedicated to protecting the implementation of FCTC from tobacco industry

[83] WHO FCTC, Fourth session, Punta del Este, 2010. *Applications for the status of observer to the Conference of the Parties to the WHO Framework Convention on Tobacco Control*, 2

[84] WHO FCTC, Fifth session, Seoul, 2012. *Economically sustainable alternatives to tobacco growing. Report by the working group.*

[85] WHO FCTC, Sixth session, Moscow, 2014. *Provisional Agenda Item 4.5.*

[86] WHO FCTC, Sixth session, Moscow, 2014. *Verbatim Records Of Plenary Meetings*, 14.

interference' was allowed to address the Conference.[87]

Taxation experts

At its 2015 meeting in Moscow, the Parties committed to large increase in taxes on cigarettes without discussion with, or the presence of, a single finance minister. Adding to this refusal to call on other interested parties, and perhaps conscious that it was seeking income from tobacco sales, the Parties barred accredited journalists from the room.[88] When the European Union failed to agree to measures that would increase taxes in 2012, the unelected Secretariat named and shamed the entire EU, awarding it a 'Dirty Ashtray', saying:

The EU has shown a lack of respect for other members of the Working Group by not taking seriously the important contributions of the other Parties and by focusing exclusively on the compromises that relate to the EU member states as opposed to the rest if the world ... it is absolutely unacceptable for Parties to attempt to link tax increases and tax rates to illicit trade.[89]

More recently, the Secretariat circulated a *Note Verbale* to Parties and NGOs.

It has come to the attention of the Convention Secretariat that some parties to the convention are being propositioned by

---

[87] WHO FCTC, Sixth Session Moscow, 2014. *Verbatim Records Of Plenary Meetings*, 98.

[88] Drew Johnson and Alex Swoyer, 'UN approves increased global tobacco tax during secret session.' *The Washington Times* 14 October 2014.

[89] *Framework Convention Alliance Bulletin,* Issue 120 25 November 2012.

tobacco companies to conclude agreements by which the companies would assume certain responsibilities and controlling the tobacco supply chain…

Furthermore, the International Tax and Investment Center, which works to further the interests of the tobacco industry … continues to organise regional and global meetings and to invite governments of parties to the [Convention]. … These meetings feature discussions on tobacco taxation… rather than the recommendations of the guidelines on implementation of Article 6 of the Convention.

The head of the Convention secretariat wishes to express her concern over these developments, and to advise parties that such behaviour is damaging for tobacco control efforts worldwide … the head of the Convention secretariat wishes to recall Article 5.3 of the Convention, which requires parties to protect public health policies on Tobacco control from commercial and other vested interests.[90]

In addition to misrepresenting Article 6 and Article 5.3, the *Note Verbale* was an appeal to States and NGOs to 'maintain solidarity' more suited to a member of the Socialist International than an international public servant.

---

[90] WHO FCTC, 'Industry interference in tracking and tracing tobacco products.' *Note Verbale* Geneva 4 March 2016. A note verbale is a diplomatic communication that is prepared in the third person and unsigned: it is less formal than a note and more formal than an aide memoire.

Media

At the Moscow conference, the Secretariat spent 40,000 GBP on Wi-Fi for journalists, which it then banned from covering the conference.[91] Indeed, all members of the public were excluded: 'COP would like to exclude all members of the public from the meeting during this COP.'[92]

The question of access to the media and the public will be further considered at COP 7, following the failure of an Australian proposal to settle the matter by a proposal of screening against 'tobacco industry' operatives at COP 6.[93] [Although Australia has not ratified the Protocol, it publishes the fact of all meetings held with the industry. Public notification of meetings between the Australian Government Department of Health and the Tobacco Industry is made through the Department of Health website, the latest is for 9 March 2016.[94]]

---

[91] Marco Giannangelli, '"Broke" WHO host £1.6 million caviar-fuelled beano.' *Express* 26 October 2014.

[92] WHO FCTC, Sixth session Moscow, 2014. *Verbatim Records of Plenary Meetings*, 28.

[93] WHO FCTC, Sixth session Moscow, 2014, *Verbatim Records of Plenary Meetings*, 18.

[94] Australian Government Department of Health, http://www.health. gov.au/internet/main/publishing.nsf/Content/tobacco-conv-public accessed 15 July 2016.

IV

About the Author

Hon Dr Gary Johns is a member of the *Australian Prime Minister's Community Business Partnership*, a director of the *Australian Institute for Progress*, a director of *DonorInform Limited*, and president of *Recognise What?*

Gary served in the House of Representatives from 1987-1996 and was Special Minister of State and Assistant Minister for Industrial Relations from 1993-1996. He served as an Associate Commissioner of the Commonwealth Productivity Commission 2002-2004.

He received the Centenary Medal and the 2002 Fulbright Professional Award in Australian-United States Alliance Studies, served at Georgetown University Washington DC.

He was Senior Fellow Institute of Public Affairs, senior consultant ACIL Tasman, Associate Professor, Australian Catholic University, and is Visiting Fellow at Queensland University of Technology Business School.

He holds a Doctor of Philosophy (Political Science) University of Queensland, Master of Arts (Geography)

Monash University, and a Bachelor of Economics Monash University.

Gary is also a columnist for *The Australian* and *The Spectator*.

His Recent books include:

Aboriginal Self-Determination (2011)

Right Social Justice (2012)

Really Dangerous Ideas (2013)

Recognise What? (2014)

The Charity Ball (2014)

No Contraception, No Dole (2015)

All books are available from:

www.connorcourt.com

V

About the Australian Institute for Progress

The Australian Institute for Progress exists to advance the discussion, development and implementation of public policy for Australia's future, from its base in Brisbane. It is politically unaligned, and funded through membership, donations and consultancies.

The AIP promotes the classic rights – freedom of expression, freedom of association, property rights, freedom of worship, and freedom of markets. It is the view of the AIP that human ingenuity is indomitable and lies at the heart of human progress. We believe that individuals – not governments – are best placed to direct their own futures, and that it is their ideas and efforts that help shape a collective future.

The AIP will contribute to debate by enabling the publication of discussion and policy papers, conduct seminars, participate in forums, and the media. We will seek to engage all Australians, but particularly those in the prime of their careers who will bear the responsibility for advancing our nation in the decades ahead of us. In this way, we will place ourselves at the centre of sensible, visionary public debate and policy discussion in Australia. We will play a leading role in helping to shape the nation we can become.

Lightning Source UK Ltd.
Milton Keynes UK
UKHW01f1803231018
331070UK00009B/308/P